Dealing with
Disorders and Disease

Cystic Fibrosis

CHERITON
CHILDREN'S BOOKS

Published in 2025 by **Cheriton Children's Books**
1 Bank Drive West, Shrewsbury, Shropshire, SY3 9DJ

First Edition

Author: Sarah Eason
Designer: Paul Myerscough
Editor: Jennifer Sanderson
Proofreader: Ellie James

Picture credits: Cover illustration by Doodle Press. Inside: p4: Shutterstock/Andrey Popov, p6: Shutterstock/Lisanne Versteeg, p7: Shutterstock/Kateryna Kon, p8: Shutterstock/Explode, p9: Shutterstock/Lightspring, p10: Shutterstock/Nazarova Mariia, p11: Shutterstock/TommyStockProject, p12: Shutterstock/Monkey Business Images, p15: AdobeStock/Rawpixel.com, p17: Shutterstock/Prostock Studio, p18: Shutterstock/Chris Harwood, p19: Shutterstock/Kateryna Kon, p20: Shutterstock/Gorodenkoff, p21: Shutterstock/Gopixa, p22b: Shutterstock/Jake Pixo, p22t: Shutterstock/Fizkes, p23: Shutterstock/WiP Studio, p24: Shutterstock/Gorodenkoff, p26: Shutterstock/UnoL, p28: Shutterstock/Chang Pooh24, p29: Shutterstock/Evgeniia Zakharishcheva, p30: Shutterstock/Thala Bhula, p32: Shutterstock/Picture Partners, p34: Shutterstock/Peakstock, p35: Shutterstock/Saiful52, p36: Shutterstock/Billion Photos, p37: Shutterstock/Frame Stock Footage, p38: Shutterstock/Andrey Popov, p39: Shutterstock/Sakurra, p41: Shutterstock/Alexander_Safonov, p42: Shutterstock/Fizkes, p43: AdobeStock/Mediteraneo, p45b: Shutterstock/Karelnoppe, p45t: Shutterstock/Pixel Shot, p46: Shutterstock/KieferPix, p47: AdobeStock/Sofiko14, p48: Shutterstock/Stokkete, p51: Shutterstock/Paulaphoto, p52: Shutterstock/Smeerjewegproducties, p53: Shutterstock/Evgeniia Zakharishcheva, p54l: Shutterstock/ESB Professional, p54r: Shutterstock/Kateryna Onyshchuk, p55: Shutterstock/Wavebreakmedia, p56: Shutterstock/Gorodenkoff, p59: Shutterstock/Andrey Popov.

Disclaimer: The photographs shown in this book are intended to support the factual content. The publisher notes that the individuals shown in the photographs do not necessarily have the condition/s described in the book.

Printed in China

Please visit our website,
www.cheritonchildrensbooks.com
to see more of our high-quality books.

Contents

CHAPTER 1

Understanding Cystic Fibrosis

Most of us have colds now and then, and our noses and throats feel blocked up. We may cough and wheeze, and might feel a bit short of breath. Occasionally, after eating particular foods, we might feel a bit nauseous or constipated or even lose our appetite. Although these symptoms can be annoying, most of us soon feel better. But people who have cystic fibrosis have many of these symptoms for some or almost all of the time.

What Is Cystic Fibrosis?

Cystic fibrosis is a disease in which the lungs and digestive system become clogged up so that they do not function properly. When lungs struggle, a person becomes unwell. For example, they take in air less efficiently, so they may struggle to get enough oxygen from air into the blood system. This gas is essential for respiration, which is when we breathe in oxygen and breathe out carbon dioxide. The digestive system is all about taking in and processing food, on a journey through the mouth, stomach, and intestines. When this system of organs is not working properly, people struggle to get the nutrients they need to keep healthy. That's why cystic fibrosis has a big impact on the lives of people with the condition.

"Cystic fibrosis causes a wide range of challenging symptoms that affect the entire body."

Passing on a Condition

Some conditions are inherited. This means that people get the condition from genes passed on from their parents, who got the genes from their parents, and so on. Genes are vital instruction codes that are found in the cells of living things. The instructions tell cells how to grow and survive, what to make that is useful for the body, and many other things. If the genes give wrong instructions, the body may malfunction, or not work properly. This is the case with cystic fibrosis, which is a type of genetic disease.

You probably know someone with cystic fibrosis because it is relatively common. Some sources say around 160,000 people have cystic fibrosis, but others say there are only around 70,000 to 165,000 cases worldwide. In the United States, around 30,000 people have cystic fibrosis and 1 in 30 Americans is a carrier. In this book, we will look at what causes cystic fibrosis, how it can be treated, and what it is like to live with this condition.

People with cystic fibrosis often need help with breathing and may need to use an inhaler from time to time.

The Role of Mucus

To understand the changes that happen in the body when someone has cystic fibrosis, it is important to know about the role of mucus. You probably know this slippery, sticky substance best as snot. When you have a cold, the nose can stream with mucus and you may cough up some. Mucus is vitally important, not only in your nose and other parts of the respiratory system, but also in other parts of the body.

Mucus in the Lungs

Mucus helps keep our lungs healthy so we can breathe. Air enters the lungs through a network of tubes including the trachea and bronchi. Along with gases, air brings in bits of dirt and dust and also living things such as bacteria and fungi that can cause harm. Cells lining the airways produce mucus that traps any small solid particles, or bits, that we breathe in. To stop the mucus from building up and blocking tubes, tiny structures called cilia on the cells sweep away the mucus and its trapped particles. Cilia are a little like microscopic hairs that move side to side like mini oars. The mucus travels slowly up the airways into the throat. Some mucus gets swallowed and some goes up to the nose, so the body can get rid of it.

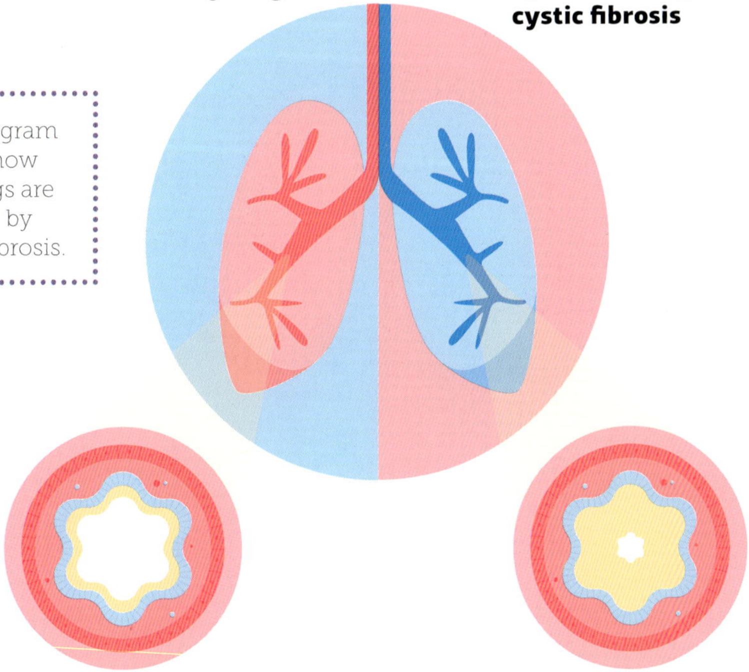

This diagram shows how the lungs are affected by cystic fibrosis.

Mucus in the Digestive System

In the mouth, esophagus, and intestines, mucus has another job: making food slippery so it moves through the digestive system. When we mash up food in our mouths, mucus in saliva (spit) mixes with chopped food to make a slippery paste that's easy to swallow. In the stomach, food is digested by powerful stomach fluids and enzymes from organs such as the pancreas. Mucus from stomach cells is essential in keeping the digestive fluids moving into the stomach and in preventing the stomach from digesting its own walls. Once the partly digested food moves out of the stomach, mucus in the intestines keeps it moving until it is fully digested. It is then excreted when we go to the toilet.

Understanding Cystic Fibrosis

People with cystic fibrosis have cells that produce a lot of thick, sticky mucus. This is a result of a problem with a protein in their cells that controls the flow of water and salts in and out. When the protein does not work properly, salts get blocked and mucus is made with less water in it, so it is thicker. With thicker mucus, cilia in lungs cannot work as well, meaning that airways can get clogged easily. Infections can happen when bacteria and viruses get trapped in the airways. Instead of protecting the digestive system, mucus clogs and blocks its functions.

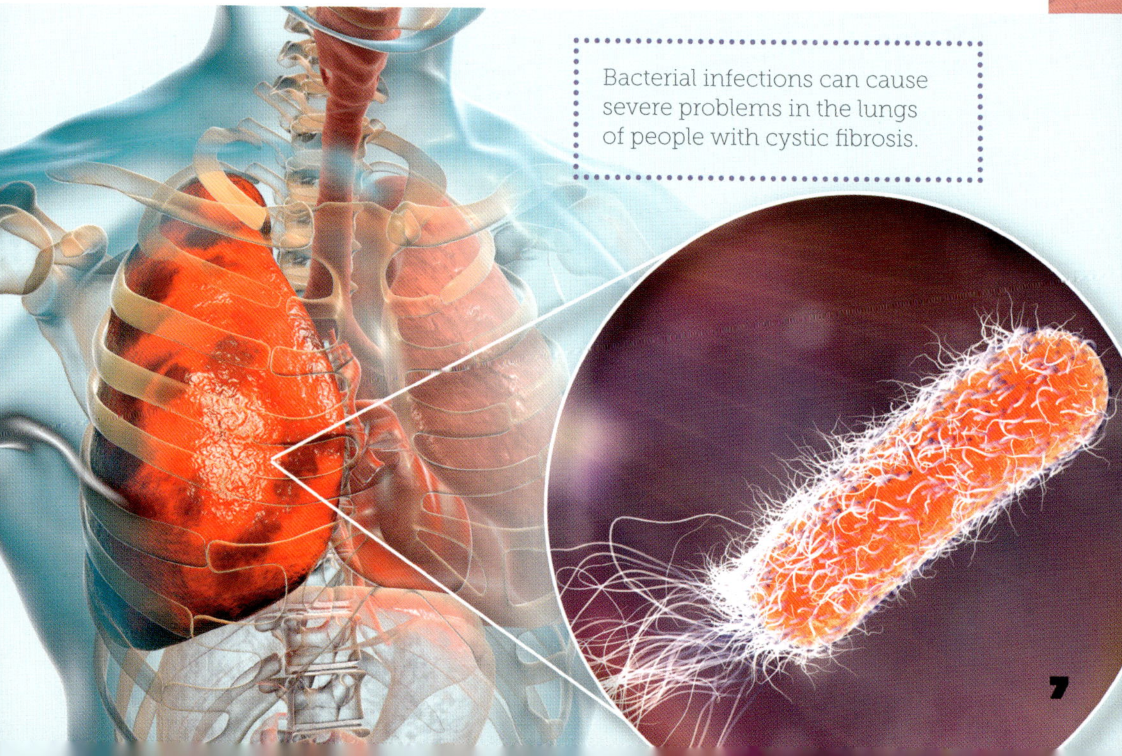

Bacterial infections can cause severe problems in the lungs of people with cystic fibrosis.

Signs of Cystic Fibrosis

People with cystic fibrosis experience a wide range of symptoms associated with the disease. The symptoms typically start to be noticeable in early childhood. Some people develop the first symptoms as soon as they are born, whereas others don't notice them until they are adults. Symptoms can get better or worse with age.

Problems in the Lungs

People with cystic fibrosis have frequent, often long-lasting bacterial and viral chest infections. As a result, they often feel poorly and have persistent coughs and stuffy noses. People with the condition often wheeze when breathing, especially during exercise when the body needs to take in more air.

Problems in the Pancreas

Tubes from the pancreas become blocked so the pancreas cannot release its digestive enzymes into the stomach. This buildup of enzymes can cause pancreatic infections and scarring that can reduce the pancreas's ability to make insulin. Insulin regulates the blood's sugar level. People who cannot regulate sugar with their own insulin are diabetic. Around 50 percent of adults with cystic fibrosis are diabetic, too.

Problems in the Gut

People with cystic fibrosis may have a poor appetite and struggle to gain weight as a result of their bodies' inability to properly digest and release nutrients from their food. Digesting fatty foods is particularly difficult. This is a reason why people with cystic fibrosis often produce greasy, foul-smelling stools (solid waste). Other digestive symptoms include a swollen abdomen (belly), nausea, diarrhea, and constipation.

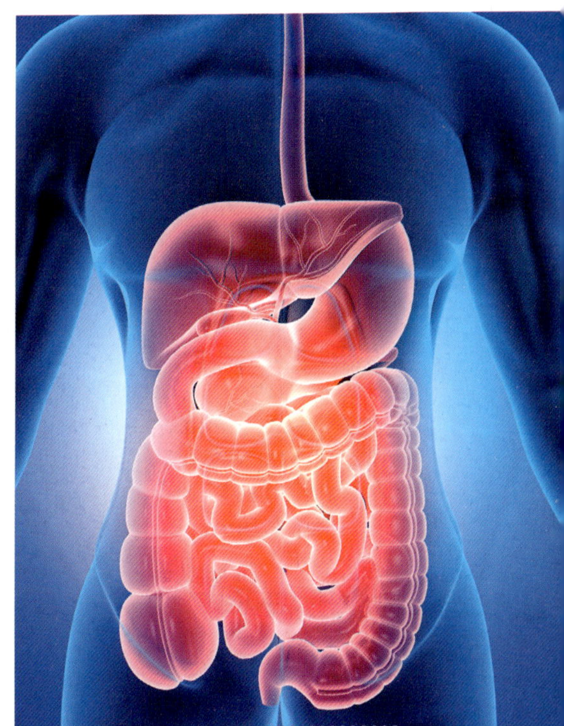

In a healthy digestive system, food breaks down easily, nutrients are absorbed, and waste is passed through the body.

Understanding Cystic Fibrosis

Many people with cystic fibrosis have nasal polyps. These are soft growths in their noses that can cause nasal congestion, pain, or loss of smell. The polyps form as a result of blocked airways and infections. Sinuses are air-filled spaces in our skulls between the eyes that help warm and moisten the air we breathe in. People with cystic fibrosis get clogged sinuses due to a buildup of mucus, which can cause pain.

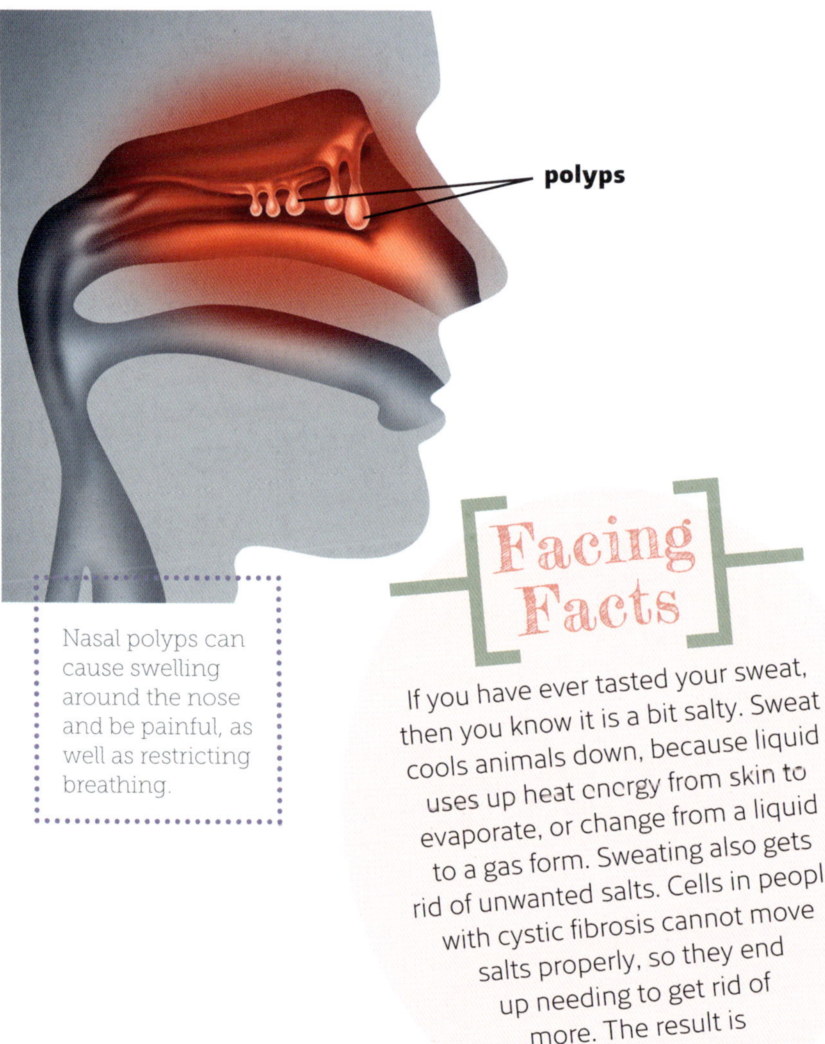

Nasal polyps can cause swelling around the nose and be painful, as well as restricting breathing.

Facing Facts

If you have ever tasted your sweat, then you know it is a bit salty. Sweat cools animals down, because liquid uses up heat energy from skin to evaporate, or change from a liquid to a gas form. Sweating also gets rid of unwanted salts. Cells in people with cystic fibrosis cannot move salts properly, so they end up needing to get rid of more. The result is very salty sweat.

Education and Cystic Fibrosis

For a young person with cystic fibrosis, going to school or college can be very difficult. People with cystic fibrosis need daily treatments and therapies to manage their condition, including airway clearance techniques, medication, and help with diet and supplements. Balancing treatments with school or college can be very tricky.

TIREDNESS AND LOST HOURS

Cystic fibrosis can make people incredibly tired. The body's energy is being spent on breathing and fighting infections, with little left over for anything else. The draining tiredness can make attending classes regularly very difficult, let alone taking part in extracurricular activities or completing homework deadlines. Many students will also need to spend time in the hospital if they get a respiratory infection and their health worsens. That and the exhausting nature of the disease means many children and young adults miss significant periods of time at school or college.

Handwashing is important for everyone to try and reduce the spread of germs, but if there is a student with cystic fibrosis present in a school or college, classmates are encouraged to be extra careful about washing their hands.

RESPIRATORY PROBLEMS MADE WORSE

The respiratory problems experienced by people with cystic fibrosis can interfere with their school or college life when they can attend. Coughing, wheezing, and feeling short of breath can make it very difficult to listen to instructions and pay attention in class. There is also the additional risk of being exposed to particles in the air in school environments that can make breathing difficulties even worse. Often, students with cystic fibrosis need to sit at least 6 feet (2 m) away from other students to reduce the risk of infection.

Time to Eat

Children and young people with cystic fibrosis often need to eat high-calorie meals and snacks throughout the day. Building that into the school day and making sure the food is available is an additional stress for students and often involves losing some study time.

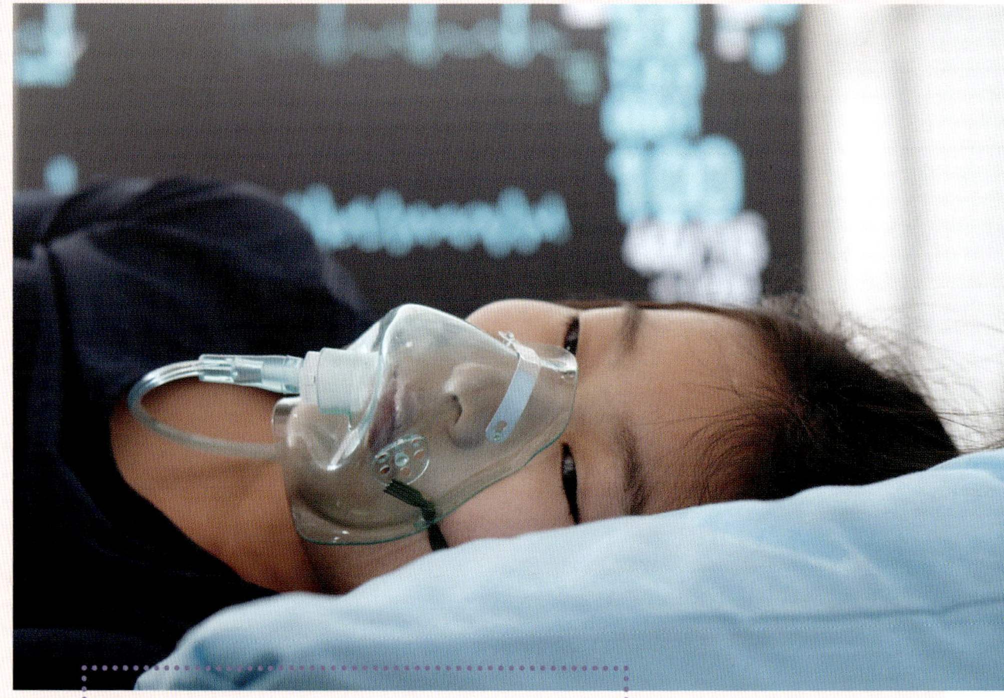

Time spent in the hospital due to infections is not only draining both emotionally and physically, it also means lost study time.

MANAGING MEDICATION

Children with cystic fibrosis usually need many different medications and treatments every day. They include medication that must be inhaled and enzymes to help with digestion. Finding time to take the medication within school hours requires a lot of planning, and support from school staff.

Dealing with Education

Although there is no doubt that having cystic fibrosis makes getting an education very difficult, it is possible. Today, educators are trained to understand the difficulties of the disease and help students find going to school or college as easy as possible. Cystic fibrosis affects everybody differently, so by discussing the student's experience of the disease with them, the best plan can be put in place.

KEEPING LEARNING FLEXIBLE

Adaptations around learning really help young people with cystic fibrosis. That can include a flexible timetable that accommodates any necessary hospital visits and time taken off school or college due to illness. Flexibility around attendance can mean students have more time at home and a lighter timetable. Today, teachers and support staff at schools and colleges work closely with students with cystic fibrosis to create personalized learning plans. That helps students put in place a structure that works for them.

Teachers need to carefully monitor signs of illness in all students, and make sure that those with cystic fibrosis are kept at a safe distance from others who might be infectious.

KEEPING HYDRATED

Drinking plenty of water during the day is especially important for people with cystic fibrosis, who need to drink 6 to 12 fluid ounces (170 to 340 ml) of water every 20 or 30 minutes. Keeping a bottle on the desk during lessons and with them during breaks makes it possible for people with cystic fibrosis to keep hydrated. Students may also need to eat during class so that they take in enough calories and nutrients throughout the day.

MEETING NEEDS

Making sure that school and college campuses are accessible for people with limited mobility helps those with cystic fibrosis. That may include elevators to different floors. Ensuring there is somewhere for any treatments also helps students, such as providing available restrooms and places in which medication or therapy can be given.

Encouraging other students to be extra-vigilant about personal hygiene helps students with cystic fibrosis. Blowing noses with a tissue and then putting it in a bin helps contain infection, as does handwashing and avoiding sharing utensils or drinking straws.

Educating other students about cystic fibrosis helps them better understand what it is like for students with the disease, and encourages them to be supportive.

CHAPTER 2

Why Cystic Fibrosis Happens

Inheriting something means having traits passed down to you by your parents. When your parents got together and had you, you inherited a blend of the genes in the cells of their bodies. People can only get cystic fibrosis if they inherit the genes that cause it from their parents.

Inheriting Genes

Many people would say the things they inherit from their parents are, for example, hair or eye color, being tall or short, or the ability to roll their tongue. The job of genes is to store coded instructions that tell cells and organs to make proteins that affect everything from the color of your hair to how you grow and your health. Remarkably, every cell in a human body contains a complete set of these genetic instructions, stored in the chromosomes in the nucleus, or center, of each cell.

Billions of Chemicals

Humans have 23 pairs of chromosomes. Each one is an X-shaped object made up of a special chemical called DNA. Up close, DNA looks a little bit like a twisted ladder with rungs containing sequences of chemicals. In total, a set of human chromosomes contains around 3 billion chemicals. We can think of a chromosome a little like a volume of an encyclopedia with thousands of entries or topics made up of billions of letters. Each gene is like a different topic.

"People have cystic fibrosis because they have inherited a faulty gene from both of their parents."

The genes we inherit from our parents are inherited from their parents, and so on.

A Combination of Genes

Each pair of chromosomes is made up of one copy of a chromosome from the mother and one from the father. Male sperm and female eggs each contain just 1 copy of each chromosome, or just 23 chromosomes in total. During sexual reproduction, a sperm fertilizes, or joins with, an egg cell and the chromosomes from each combine to make pairs. The embryo that develops from the fertilized egg contains 23 pairs of chromosomes, or one copy of each encyclopedia of genes.

Understanding Cystic Fibrosis

No two people, not even identical twins, are exactly alike. Our differences are due to very slight variations in the genetic code, a bit like small spelling changes, rewordings, or text rearrangements in the encyclopedias. Usually when genes or the proteins they make differ, individuals may look different but the genes and proteins work correctly, so there is no impact on health. However, the genetic changes sometimes have a big impact on health, as is the case with cystic fibrosis.

Changes in the Genes

You probably think of the word "mutated" as meaning something artificially changed and gone wrong. In fact, mutations are a normal part of the way genes and chromosomes slightly change over time.

Genetic Mutations

Some mutations can be beneficial to individuals and even to whole animal species. For example, in the distant past, some giraffe relatives had gene mutations that made their necks extra long. This trait enabled them to reach the leaves of tall trees. They could get more to eat, so they were more likely to survive than giraffes with shorter necks. They passed that gene to their descendants. Over time, the species changed until all giraffes were born with long necks. However, not all mutations are helpful. Some are bad. In people with cystic fibrosis, mutations in a gene disrupt the normal production and functioning of a protein found in cells in the lungs, digestive system, and other body parts.

Carrying the Gene

More than 10 million Americans carry a mutation in the cystic fibrosis gene but do not have the disease. This is the case because these people have only one copy of the mutation. People only have cystic fibrosis if they inherit two copies of the mutation—one from each parent. How does this work? Cystic fibrosis is a recessive disorder. That means that in people with mixed genes, the activity of the healthy copy masks the activity of the faulty copy. So these people produce normal mucus, have fewer lung infections, and so on. They are said to be cystic fibrosis carriers, but they do not actually suffer from the disease. The situation would be different if cystic fibrosis was a dominant mutation.

Dominant mutations are expressed when there is only one copy in a chromosome. For example, people have brown eyes if they have one brown mutation of the eye color gene, because this mutation is dominant over other eye colors.

Understanding Cystic Fibrosis

Doctors talk about the percentage chance of children inheriting diseases such as cystic fibrosis. Each individual baby has the same chance of inheriting cystic fibrosis mutations from both parents, regardless of whether their siblings have it.

Child of two carriers of the mutated cystic fibrosis gene:

- One in four, or 25 percent, chance that the child will not be a carrier
- One in four, or 25 percent, chance that the child will have cystic fibrosis
- Two in four, or 50 percent, chance that the child will be a carrier

Child of two people, one with cystic fibrosis and the other a carrier:

- Two in four, or 50 percent, chance that the child will be a carrier
- Two in four, or 50 percent, chance that the child will have cystic fibrosis

The Cystic Fibrosis Gene

The gene responsible for cystic fibrosis is formally named cystic fibrosis transmembrane conductance regulator, or CFTR for short. CFTR is a part of the long arm of chromosome 7 in humans, which is just one of 23 different chromosomes in the human genome. The CFTR gene contains instructions to make a wiggly protein called CFTR made up of nearly 1,500 amino acids. One job of this protein is to create special gates in certain cell walls that control how much salt and water are let through. Such gates are found in cells that make mucus, saliva, sweat, tears, and digestive enzymes. The CFTR protein also regulates other channels in cells whose proper functioning is important for normal function of the pancreas and lungs.

When we cry, special gates in cell walls have allowed fluid to pass through.

More than One Mutation

Scientists know that it is not just one type of mutation in CFTR causing the symptoms of cystic fibrosis. There are well over 1,700 different variants, or mutations, of the CFTR gene. However, nearly all cases of the disease in the United States and two-thirds of cases worldwide are caused by a single variant called Delta F508. In this mutation, a slip-up of just three code letters in the gene cause CFTR proteins to be produced by cells that lack just one amino acid. This fault is enough to prevent the protein from working properly.

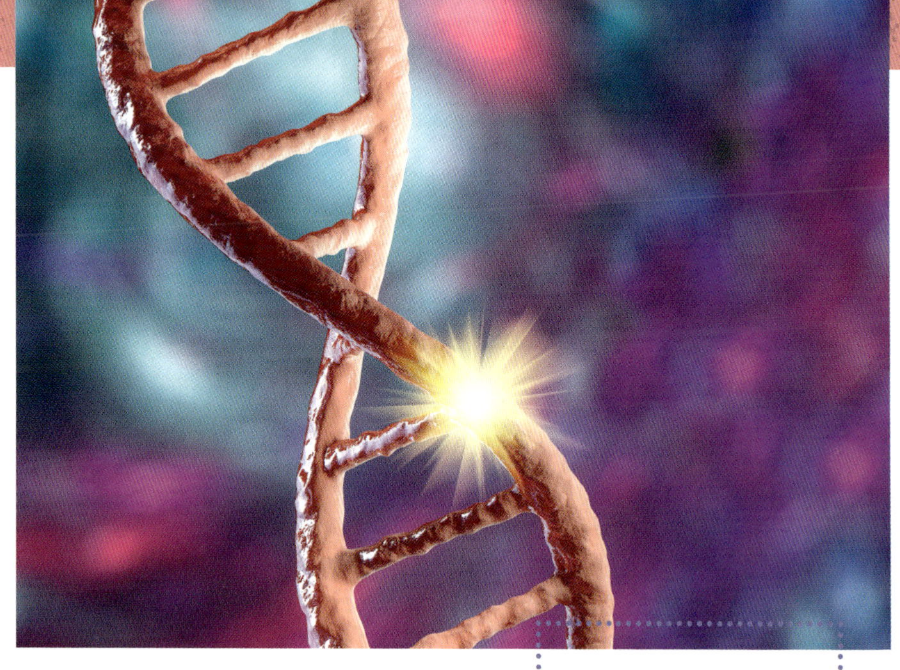

Cystic fibrosis is caused by a mutation in the CFTR gene.

Understanding Cystic Fibrosis

Many different variants and combinations of variants can cause different disease symptoms. For example, people with some variants are more likely to have pancreatic problems, whereas those with other variants often have more lung problems. Still other variants in CFTR seem to have no effect on health and so do not cause cystic fibrosis. Not all patients with the same variants have the same symptoms, partly because other genes affect the disease. For example, mutations in a gene called mannan-binding lectin can make bacterial lung infections in people with cystic fibrosis more likely, no matter what CFTR variant they have.

Facing Facts

The severity of cystic fibrosis symptoms can vary widely depending on the specific CFTR mutations a person inherits. Some mutations result in milder forms of the disease with fewer respiratory and digestive complications, while others lead to more severe disease with more debilitating symptoms.

Treating the Gene

People with cystic fibrosis can face a lifetime of medication and physical therapy to keep their symptoms under control, so they can lead normal lives. However, in the near future, new techniques may be available to treat the mutations in the CFTR gene in patients with the disease. This could help their cells to make the CFTR protein properly and produce normal mucus. The new treatments are called gene therapy.

Understanding Gene Therapy

When an automobile is not working, a mechanic may remove and replace the faulty part so it works again. The idea of gene therapy is similar. Scientists find the section of DNA forming a gene that is not functioning properly and replace it with a new, functioning gene.

How Scientists Identify Genes

Scientists have so far identified around 21,000 genes in humans, each with a different job to do on its own or in combination with other genes. They have a better idea than ever before of where they need to make gene changes on chromosomes to improve health. Gene therapy has been successful in treating some conditions, such as sickle-cell disease.

Facing Facts

It is only in recent times that better laboratory techniques and improved equipment, such as powerful computers, have become available for scientists to use. That has revolutionized the study of genes.

Gene therapy was first developed in the 1970s. Since then, our understanding of genetics has become far more advanced.

Editing the Genes

When an essay has spelling mistakes or parts that don't make sense, we edit and correct it. One type of gene therapy is called gene editing because it uses special techniques to edit and correct the faulty coding in DNA. The main technique, called CRISPR/Cas9, uses a tiny piece of DNA with a chemical code that matches that of the section of DNA sequence that needs to be edited. It binds to this section so that a protein called Cas9, which acts like scissors, can cut out exactly the right part. Then scientists can cut, paste, and delete single letters of the code to make corrections.

Research into genetics is one of the most cutting-edge areas of modern science, and is likely to provide future solutions to many different disorders and diseases, including cystic fibrosis.

A Challenging Therapy

In gene therapy, the challenge is to get new genes into tiny cells. Scientists have two main ways of delivering new genes to replace mutated genes. One is through the air and the other uses unusual messengers—viruses!

If you have ever had a cold, then you have been attacked by a virus. These tiny organisms invade cells, and once inside, they use energy from this host cell to make hundreds of thousands of copies of their DNA.

Viruses are incredibly small entities, much smaller even than bacteria, which can only reproduce once they enter a living cell.

Using Viruses to Deliver Genes

Scientists use modified, or changed, viruses as a gene delivery service. In a laboratory, they remove any of the virus's own genes that can cause sicknesses in people. They then replace them with the normal-functioning gene to be added in the gene therapy procedure. Viruses enter cells with the mutated version of the gene. The normal gene from the virus "infects" the cell, replacing the mutated gene. The next step of gene therapy is to put cells with the normal gene back into the person with the condition, ideally in places where the tissue needs a helping hand. In someone with cystic fibrosis, for example, large numbers of new cells can be injected into the pancreas or intestinal wall to replace faulty genes and spread copies of the normal gene.

Understanding Cystic Fibrosis

In people with lung problems caused by cystic fibrosis, an alternative way of delivering genes is by inhaling them with a nebulizer. In this gene therapy, normal CFTR DNA is encased, or wrapped, in bubbles of fat. These bubbles travel to the lungs and deliver the DNA into cells there. In 2015, a trial tested this nebulizer delivery system. It found that when patients used this therapy monthly for a year, they had improved breathing and fewer lung infections than those who didn't.

Nebulizers help people breath, but they are now also being used to deliver gene therapy.

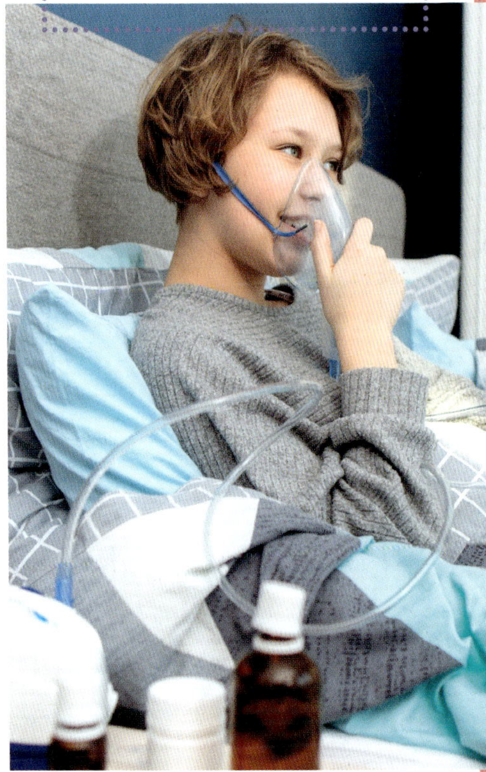

Perfecting the Therapy

Scientists, universities, drug companies, and charities for a variety of inherited diseases have spent thousands of millions of dollars globally trying to perfect gene therapy. However, only a few safe, approved therapies are actually available at present. The development process is slow because of the many challenges involved with introducing new genes into cells to keep them working.

An Immune Response

A major challenge to gene therapy is the body's immune system, which acts like a defensive shield. This system rallies white blood cells to defend other cells in the body when they detect attack by invaders such as bacteria and viruses. Injected cells containing viruses may be recognized as intruders, too. This immune response can tire people and even make them seriously sick. Doctors sometimes give patients drugs to suppress their immune system to make gene therapy more effective, although this increases a patient's risk of getting an infection.

When a new drug or therapy is developed, it is generally tested first on tissue cultures, but also on animals in laboratories.

Mixed Messages

Replacement genes should ideally integrate, or stitch themselves, into DNA on chromosomes in cells. But if the gene integrates to the wrong place on chromosomes, or in the wrong tissues, it might cause health problems for patients. For example, in the early twenty-first century, gene therapy for a rare immune disease caused blood cancer in some patients. The introduced genes had changed a gene that controls the growth speed of cells.

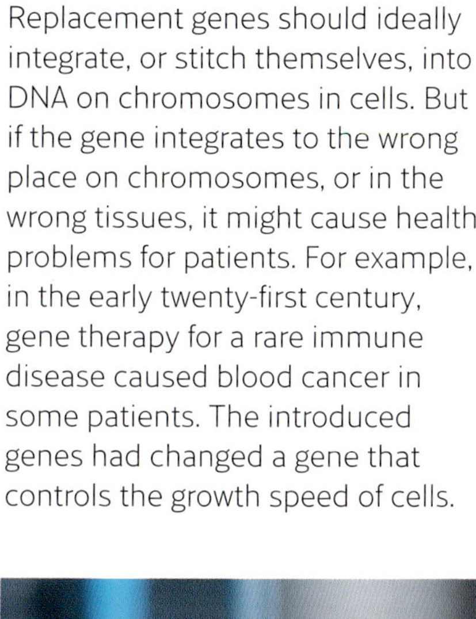

Unreliable Testing

To try out a therapy or drug, scientists usually simulate a human disorder or illness in the animals, then test therapies. But this approach cannot work with some animals. For example, if scientists introduce mutated CFTR genes into mice to give them cystic fibrosis, the mice do not get lung disease. However, pigs can get lung disease with cystic fibrosis, so they are better test animals than mice.

Understanding Cystic Fibrosis

In recent years, researchers in the United States have developed two new virus delivery systems for getting functioning CFTR into the lungs of pigs with cystic fibrosis. One used a type of virus called a lentivirus that directly integrates the CFTR into lung cells, making the change permanent. The other used different viruses, called AAV, which are easier to make in large quantities and specifically target airway cells, but cannot deliver long-lasting effects. Both gene therapies restored normal salt movement in pig airway cells. They also improved the ability of mucus to fight off bacterial infections.

Concerns about Gene Therapy

Gene therapy interferes with nature and makes changes to the body's set of basic instructions. For these reasons and others, it raises many ethical concerns. Gene therapy is very expensive because it tends to be used on small numbers of people with rare disorders. It can also take years of patient work in laboratories and testing before therapies are safe enough to go on sale. Some people fear this means such expensive therapies will only be available for wealthy people, not everyone.

Picking and Choosing Genes

In the future, gene therapies may make it possible to correct many types of mutations in people. For example, they might "fix" sex cells so that replacement, improved genes can be passed on to children, and from those children to their children. This could spare future generations from having diseases such as cystic fibrosis. However, it also might affect how fetuses develop and bring on unexpected health problems. Also, some parents might want to start specifying other gene changes, such as making their children smarter or better at sports.

Stem Cell Research

Unspecialized cells called stem cells can develop into other distinct types, such as neurons, lung cells, or muscle cells, and can also make multiple copies of themselves. One stem cell can split over and over to produce millions of cells in a body. The stem cells used for cystic fibrosis therapies usually come from bones or blood. But some stem cells come from spare, unused human embryos donated for research by the parents. Some people believe strongly that it is ethically wrong to use cells from any embryo for gene therapy.

Many physicians and scientists argue that using animals for testing is necessary. Gene therapies may harm the animals in laboratories, but this is far better than risking harm to people. Some people, however, have a major problem with harming other living things for the benefit of humans. They also argue that what works in one type of animal will not always work in people, because of their differences.

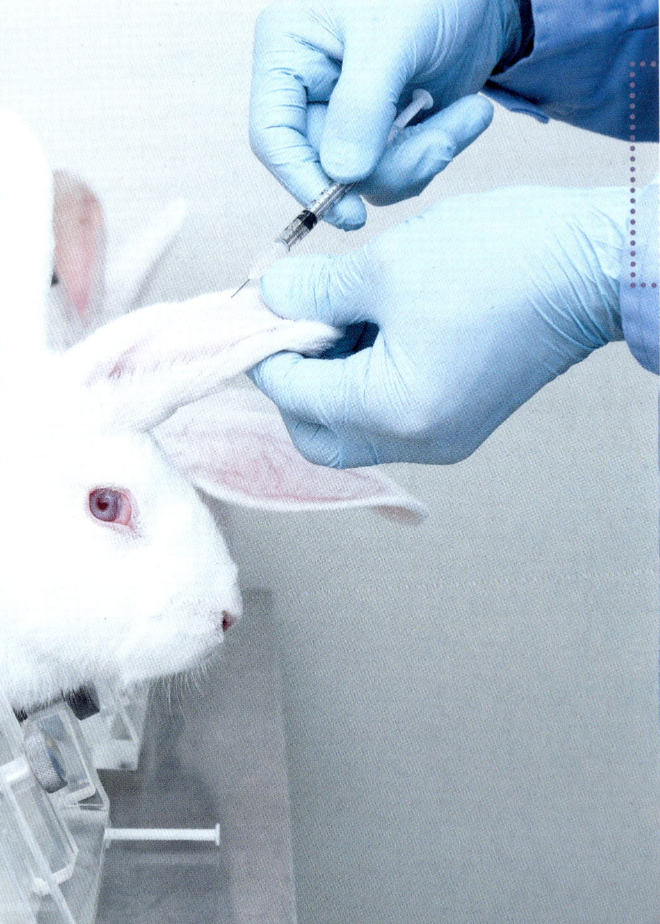

Animal testing is controversial—because it does not always prove effective and because there are concerns about animal welfare.

Social Connections and Cystic Fibrosis

Keeping up with friends and family and having fun times are important, but for people with cystic fibrosis that can be hard. The daily management of the disease often leaves very little time for anything else, so taking time out to relax and enjoy the company of other people may not be something that sufferers often get to do. However, it is a part of life that is known to improve both mental and physical health.

THE RISK OF INFECTION

Often, people with cystic fibrosis may feel anxious about spending time outside the home. The increased risk of catching an infection that can make their health even worse puts many people off going out regularly. It can be difficult to keep a distance from people when in public places, and if they are poorly ventilated, the risk of airborne germs being inhaled increases. Surfaces can be covered with germs too. Inviting people to their own home also carries a risk for people with the disease. Despite limiting the number of people contact is made with, there is always a chance one could have an infection.

After spending time in hospital due to infection, people are often fearful of catching another one and may limit contact with others.

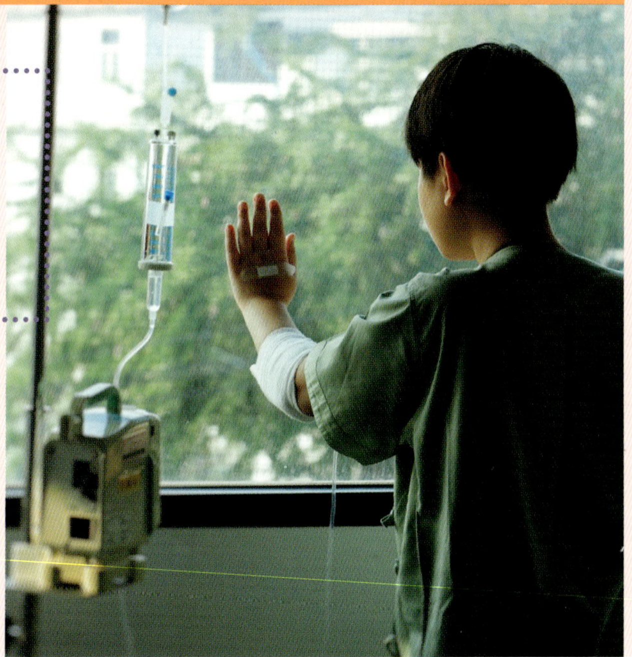

NOT ENOUGH TIME AND TOO TIRED

The daily demands of regular eating, taking supplements and medication, exercising, and healthcare appointments takes a lot of time and commitment. It can be difficult for people with cystic fibrosis to find the time—or energy—for a social life. Added to that, daily fatigue can make the thought of going out to mix with others seem completely overwhelming.

Not Able to Meet Others

People who have life-changing conditions often like to meet or form face-to-face support groups where they can talk to each other, offer advice, and share experiences. This is not possible for cystic fibrosis sufferers. People with cystic fibrosis can never meet each other, because each one has bacteria in their lungs that could be harmful to another. These bacteria grow in the lungs and are usually harmless to people who don't have the condition. But they can be easily passed from one person with cystic fibrosis to another, and they can be very harmful. This is known as cross-infection. It is such a serious risk that at conferences and other meetings about the condition, only one person with cystic fibrosis can be present at a time.

People with cystic fibrosis may worry that if they struggle with their breathing while out, other people may not react well.

Dealing with Social Connections

Managing expectations is part of life for people with cystic fibrosis, and that includes their social interactions. From the worrying risk of infection if socializing face-to-face with others through the physical exhaustion and other debilitating symptoms that come with the disease, maintaining a social life is hard. However, by adapting what they do and how they do it, people with the disease can have great relationships with family and friends.

BEING ABLE TO SAY "NO"

People with the disease need to keep a close eye on their energy levels and symptoms. If they are struggling, it is important that they feel confident about canceling plans and explaining why if people are disappointed. Being able to say "no" to social invitations or expectations is vital if fatigue and pain are severe. Thankfully, we live in an age when people can stay connected to family and friends through phone calls, video chats, and social media. If people with cystic fibrosis can't meet up with others, or are worried about doing so, they can still keep in touch online.

For young people with health conditions, missing out on social events can be very hard.

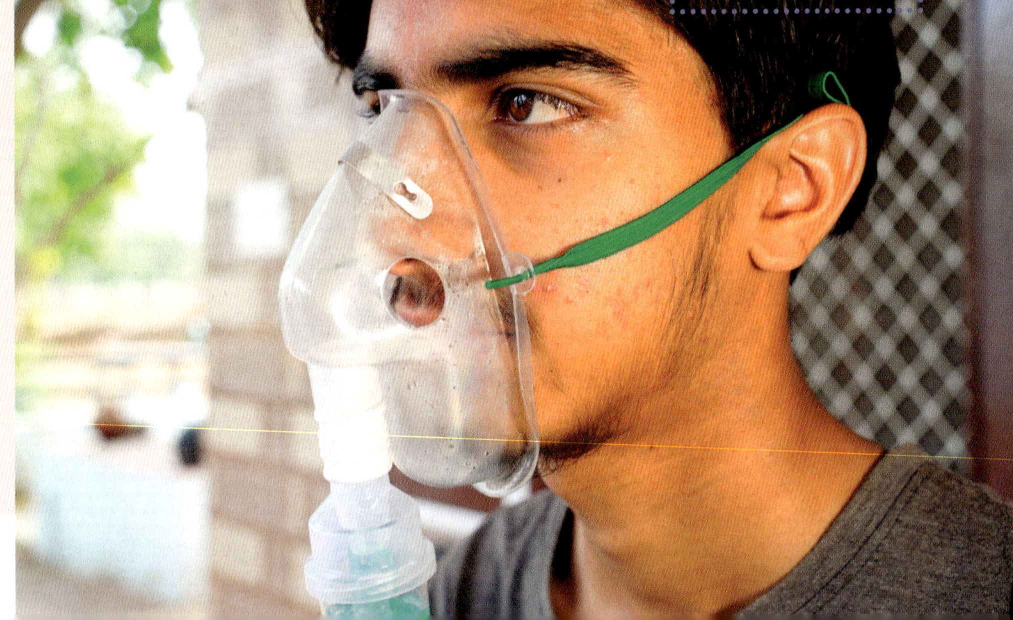

SELF-CARE FIRST

People with the condition need to plan much of their day around taking medication, getting rest, and having therapies. Those things will always need to take priority. Family will understand that is the case, because they spend time with people with the disease and know how demanding it is. However, people outside the family are usually less aware. It is often necessary to explain to friends that any meet-ups, phone calls, or events need to fit around a schedule in which care and treatment have to come first. Explaining why also helps people understand the necessary limitations.

- Social activities that fit in with self-care, such as gentle walks, yoga, swimming, and other beneficial exercise is a great way for people to keep connected with others, as long as they are well enough to take part.

- Education is key when it comes to managing chronic conditions. The better educated everyone is about chronic disease, the more accommodating they will be of those who suffer from them. Just because a person with cystic fibrosis cannot meet in person, it doesn't mean they would not love to talk on a video chat or share text messages.

CHAPTER 3

Genetics and Cystic Fibrosis

Diagnosis of cystic fibrosis can happen at any age when symptoms show up. However, two-thirds of people with the disease are diagnosed below one year of age. These diagnoses often result from routine newborn checkups. Early screening is important because even babies that seem healthy may have serious medical disorders, such as cystic fibrosis.

Testing Blood

In one test, a doctor, nurse, or midwife collects a baby's blood sample. The baby is kept warm and its sock is removed. Then the baby's heel is pricked with a lancet, which is a plastic pen-like object with a button that makes a narrow, sharp blade come out from inside and retract again. Parents or healthcare professionals usually cuddle or feed the baby while the heel stick is performed, to help distract and calm them. The heel is pressed gently to produce drops of blood that are collected on a screening card to create several dried blood spots. This card, including details of the baby's name, age, and parents, is then sent to a laboratory. Scientists analyze the blood by seeing how bacteria grow on dishes of jelly when a blood spot is added. If the blood contains certain proteins indicating diseases such as cystic fibrosis, the bacteria grow better.

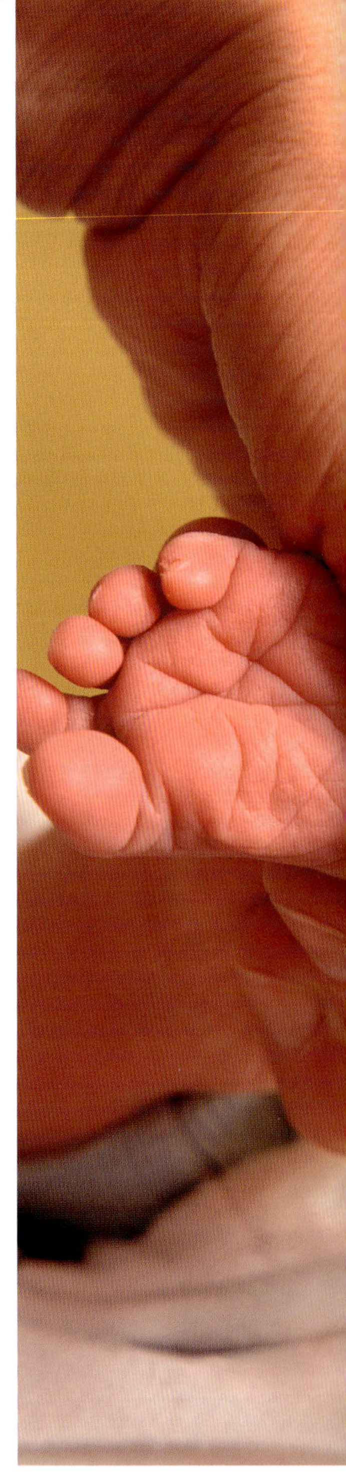

Testing for Protein

Newborn babies with cystic fibrosis have blood containing higher-than-normal amounts of a protein called trypsinogen. Trypsinogen is used to help make pancreatic enzymes, so if the pancreas is partly blocked, less of the trypsinogen will have been used up. If levels are high, there is a strong chance a baby has the disease.

Understanding Cystic Fibrosis

If someone has a history of cystic fibrosis in their family, or a child or partner with the disease, they may choose to get carrier testing to see if they carry the faulty gene that can cause the disease. They can do so with a simple mouthwash or blood test.

"Carrier testing is often done for people who are thinking about starting a family and have a relative with cystic fibrosis."

Heel prick tests are done as quickly as possible to minimize any discomfort.

Spotting a Pattern

When people feel unwell, doctors check signs of health such as temperature and pulse rate, but they also look out for signs of different diseases or disorders. People with cystic fibrosis often have a medical history of repeated respiratory and digestive problems. If a doctor notices this pattern, they may carry out tests that help confirm this possible diagnosis.

Confirming Cystic Fibrosis

Doctors may use a spirometer to help confirm cystic fibrosis. This electronic device has a breathing tube. A patient breathes in fully before pressing the lips around the mouthpiece on the tube and exhaling as hard and fully as possible. The spirometer measures how much air the patient can exhale in one second and the total amount exhaled in one forced breath. Doctors compare these measurements against normal measurements for someone of similar height, age, weight, and sex. People with cystic fibrosis may have measurements just one-half to one-third of normal spirometer readings.

Facing Facts

Sweat testing for raised salt levels is a more reliable method than blood testing, as some people can have raised trypsinogen even when they do not have cystic fibrosis. In the sweat test, a chemical is rubbed onto a small area of an arm or leg. Electrical stimulation is applied for around five minutes to encourage the sweat glands to produce sweat. A person may feel tingling in the area, or a feeling of warmth. The sweat is collected, then tested in a laboratory for its saltiness.

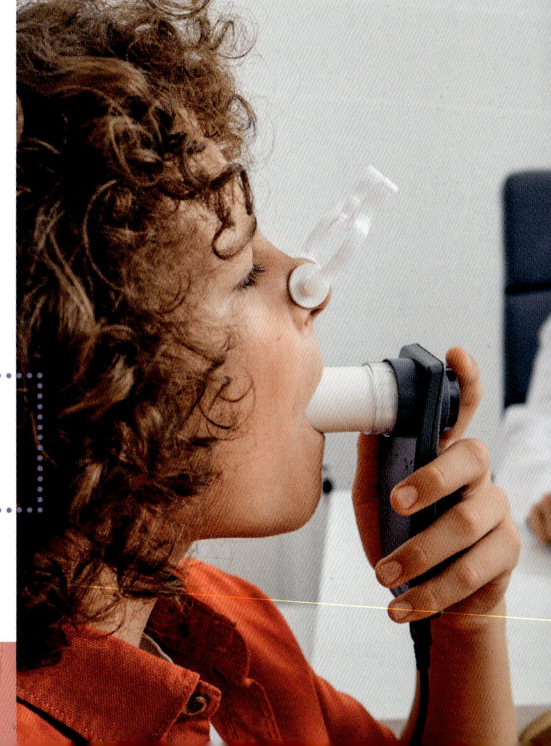

Testing with a spirometer indicates the strength and health of a person's lungs.

Understanding Cystic Fibrosis

Stool testing is another way to check for cystic fibrosis. Wearing protective gloves, patients collect a sample of their stool (solid waste) from the toilet and put it into a sample tube. This sample is then tested in a lab for levels of enzymes made by the pancreas, including elastase. If levels are unusually low in stools, it is a sign that low levels are present in the intestine, and that the pancreas is blocked. Cystic fibrosis is a common reason why this happens. It is also one explanation for higher-than-normal amounts of fat in stools, but this can be caused by eating lots of fatty foods.

This microscopic image shows fat in a stool sample. The presence of high amounts of fat in samples can be one of the signs of cystic fibrosis.

Looking Inside the Patient

Healthcare professionals can use a range of different equipment in hospitals to help diagnose and evaluate the symptoms and healthcare needs of people with cystic fibrosis. Two of the tests rely on X-rays. These are a form of invisible, high-energy radiation that can pass through soft body parts such as skin and muscle.

Using X-Rays

As an X-ray passes through a body, some of its energy is absorbed. Hard tissues such as bone absorb more energy than soft tissues or empty spaces. Machines can detect the pattern of X-rays before and after the passage to produce images of a patient's insides. X-ray imaging is important for seeing inside the lungs of patients with cystic fibrosis to discover the extent of the damage the thickened mucus is having on the lungs' function.

Evidence from X-Rays

Chest X-rays use a beam of X-rays from a fixed position. This exam produces images clear enough for specially trained health workers called radiographers to spot mucus buildup in airways. They can also see any signs of changed tissue in the walls of the lungs that could indicate a lung infection. Then doctors might prescribe antibiotics, which are medicines that treat certain infections.

An X-ray image allows doctors to see inside the lungs and search for any signs of infection.

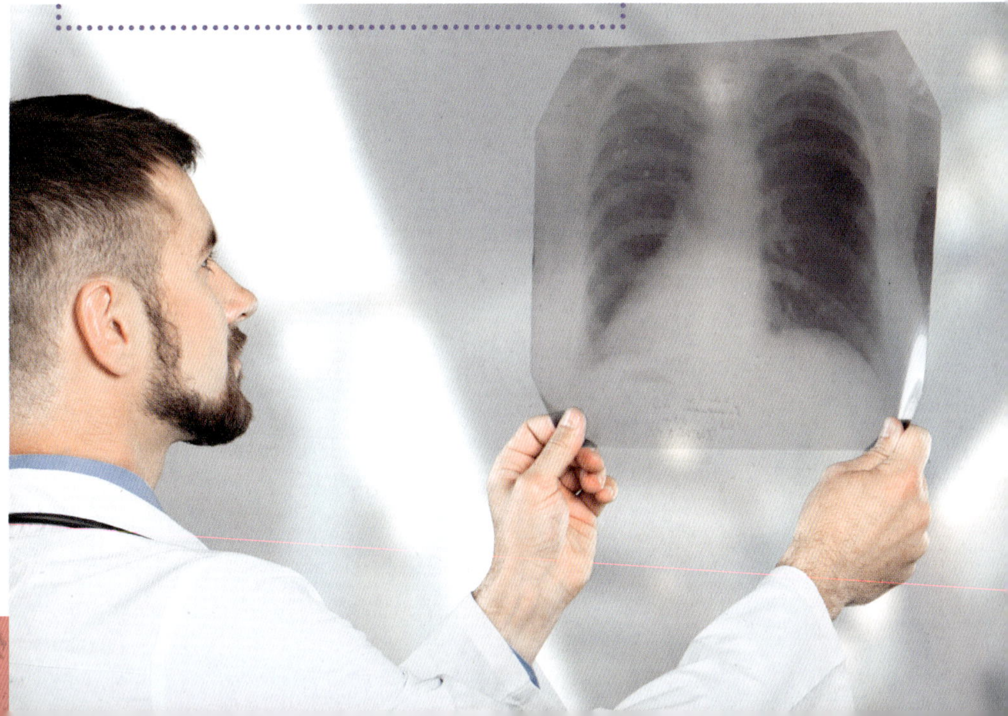

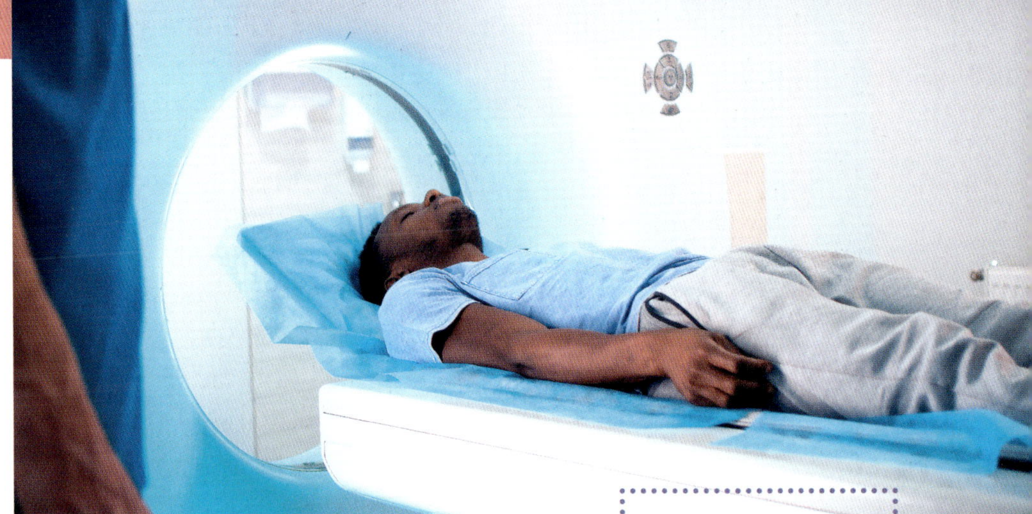

A CT scan can show the lungs, the intestines, and even blocked sinuses and polyps in the nose.

Other Forms of X-Ray Testing

Computed tomography (CT) scans expose a patient to weaker X-rays from a source moving around the patient. The patient lies down and their bed is slowly transported through a ring containing the X-ray equipment. Imaging by CT provides more detailed and higher-definition three-dimensional (3-D) imaging.

Understanding Cystic Fibrosis

Ultrasound imaging uses high-frequency sound rather than X-rays to help diagnose problems. Machinery fires pulses of ultrasound into a patient and "listens" for echoes bouncing back from the insides. It then translates the echoes into images. Ultrasound imaging is ideal for spotting blockages in the pancreas, liver, and gallbladder, organs whose functions are all affected by cystic fibrosis.

Facing Facts

Ultrasound imaging is also used to confirm a fairly rare condition called *meconium ileus* in newborn babies. With *meconium ileus*, fecal matter (solid waste) called meconium in the newborn's intestines is unusually thick and blocks the intestines, causing discomfort. Sometimes the meconium can twist the bowel and, in rare cases, cause it to split open. Most babies with this condition have cystic fibrosis.

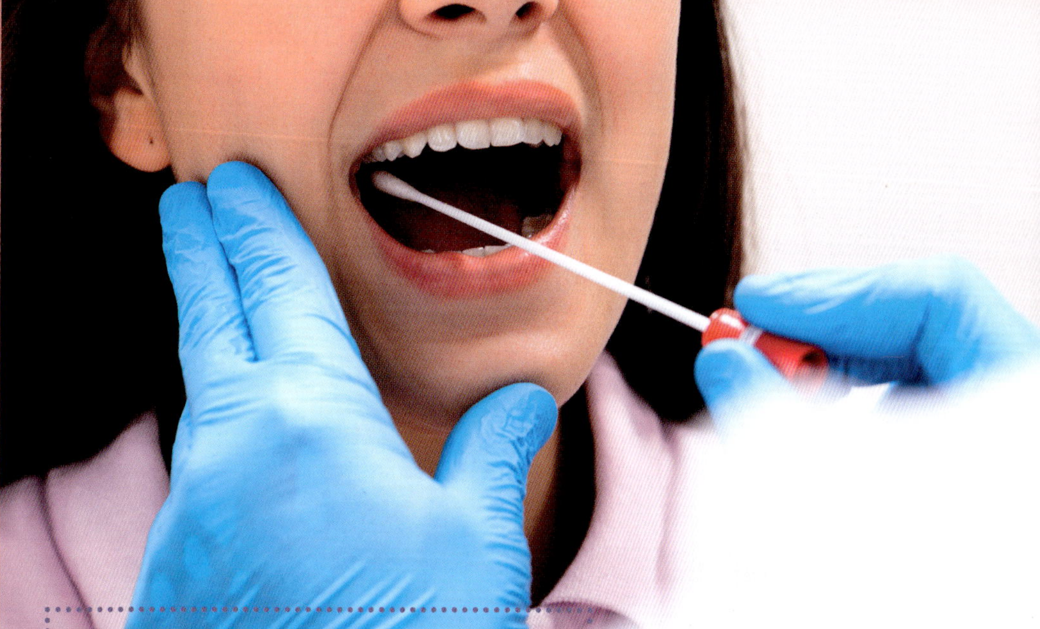

A swab test takes just seconds to perform but provides scientists with vital DNA.

Confirming the Diagnosis

Positive heel stick and sweat tests, poor spirometry performance, and problematic stool samples can all lead to a probable diagnosis of cystic fibrosis. The results of X-rays, CT scans, and ultrasounds can make the diagnosis almost certain. However, another way to confirm a diagnosis is through genetic testing. Healthcare providers order a genetic test for people suspected to have cystic fibrosis, based on other tests and signs, for two reasons. First, it can confirm whether they have a mutated CFTR gene or not. Second, it can also identify which variant they have.

Testing Cells

Laboratory workers can analyze cells from heel-stick testing and other blood tests, and cells from other sites around the body. One of the easiest places to get these cells is the mouth. Cells inside the cheek help protect the underlying tissue from being worn down, and from damage by heat and chemicals in food, by forming a loose layer of dead cells. Healthcare workers may rub a swab gently around the inside of a person's mouth to pick up cheek cells. Patients may also swish a special mouthwash around to wash away cheek cells. The swab or mouthwash is collected and the cells they contain are sent to laboratories for gene testing.

Testing Genes

The first step in reading genes is to get DNA from inside cells. Cells are put into a special detergent that splits them open by destroying membranes around the cell and nucleus. Other chemicals remove the proteins and separate the DNA from the mix. Technicians then use special techniques called DNA sequencing to read the genes in the DNA. These involve using ultrasound to break the DNA into shorter pieces. They are then treated with heat and different chemicals so computers can read the sequences of chemical codes in the genetic material. Any mutations in CFTR can be found through DNA sequencing.

Understanding Cystic Fibrosis

Carriers of the cystic fibrosis gene often want to know if their unborn child will have the disease or just be a carrier, so they will be ready to deal with the symptoms and issues as soon as the baby is born. That is why genetic tests are also performed on cells in amniotic fluid, which is the fluid that surrounds a fetus during pregnancy. The procedure to take amniotic fluid, or even cells from the umbilical cord, has to be done very carefully to avoid any possible harm to the baby or mother.

Within the uterus, a baby is fed via the umbilical cord, which is attached to a placenta. Amniotic fluid surrounds the baby.

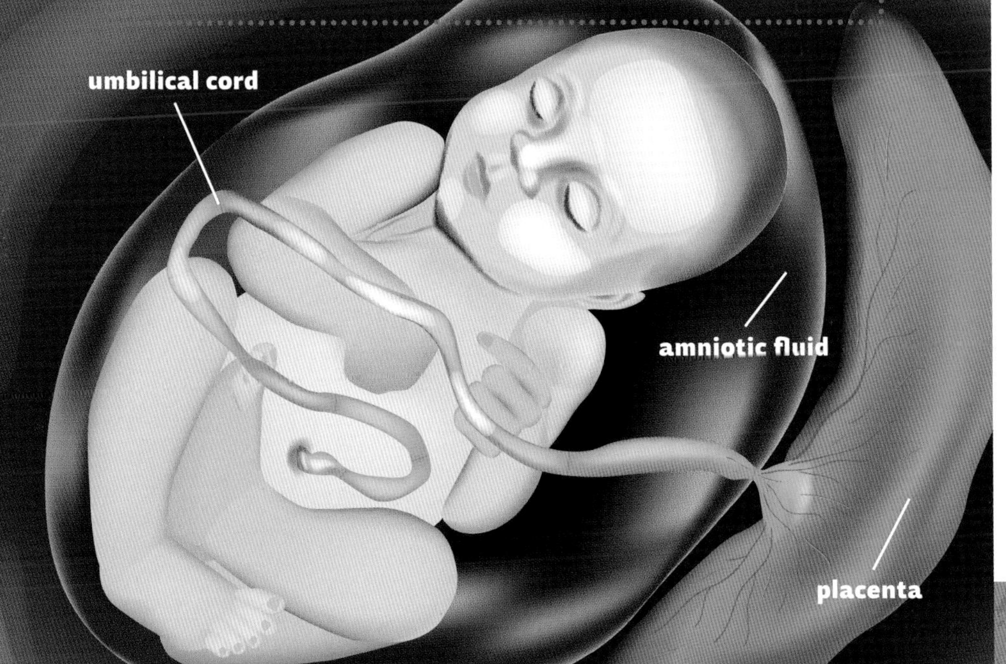

CHAPTER 4

Help with Cystic Fibrosis

People with cystic fibrosis have a wide range of treatment options that can improve their daily lives, help them deal with the more serious health problems, and reduce the chance of having severe symptoms.

Using Medication

The struggling airways and lungs of people with cystic fibrosis can get some help from a wide range of different medications. Because symptoms and severity vary in people with the condition, they need to work closely with healthcare practitioners to create a program of medications that works for them. Any program needs to be carefully monitored and changed as needed to match fluctuations, or changes, in symptoms. These are some of the medications used to treat cystic fibrosis:

Antibiotics: These are medications that kill bacteria or prevent them from reproducing or spreading. They do not work against viral infections. People with cystic fibrosis take antibiotics such as azithromycin, usually in pill form, several times per week. These medications prevent bacterial infections and airway inflammation (swelling).

Anti-inflammatory drugs:
These are medications that may be given to help reduce inflammation in the airways and improve the functioning of the lungs.

Mucus busters: Some medications help break down thick mucus so it is easier to cough up. For example, an enzyme called DNase dissolves leftover, springy DNA from dead cells in the lungs and thins the mucus in these areas. Other drugs thin the mucus by changing the balance of salt in airway cells so they suck in less water from the mucus.

Widening airways:
Bronchodilators such as Albuterol relax muscles in the airways to increase airflow to the lungs.

People with cystic fibrosis usually have to take large quantities of medication every day.

Facing Facts

Scarring and infections over time can leave some people's lungs in a very poor state. They may be so damaged that they can only manage 30 percent of their normal function. In these cases, a lung transplant is considered. This can only happen if an appropriate donor has recently died and has put their organs up for donation to the sick. Lungs need to be a match in size, age, and other factors to make a transplant most effective. There is a shortage of donor lungs, but for the lucky recipients, new healthy lungs can transform their health and their lives.

"Taking medication is a significant part of daily life for people with cystic fibrosis."

Using Physical Therapy

One of the most important ways to make sure people with cystic fibrosis feel as healthy as possible is to use physical therapy. The main objective of physical therapy is airway clearance, or getting rid of mucus buildup.

Clearing the Airways

There are many techniques for airway clearance, and people with cystic fibrosis typically do them one to four times every day.

Percussion: A person leans forward while someone, such as a relative or a healthcare worker, claps cupped hands along the sides of the chest. The cupped shape captures air that softens the blow. Like beating a drum, percussion is done with a steady beat. The blows loosen the sticky mucus in smaller airways. Vibration with a flat hand on the chest gently shakes the mucus into larger airways.

Breathing techniques: Physical therapists can teach controlled breathing in different parts of the lungs to clear them. Deep breathing is sometimes combined with huffing, coughing, and relaxed breathing to move mucus along.

Physical therapy machines: A high-frequency oscillation vest is a device that inflates and vibrates at high speed to push against the chest and help shift mucus from it. The vest mimics percussion activities. Some other machines have masks that patients wear to develop stronger exhalation, which can help clear airways.

Practicing breathing techniques can help people keep their lungs healthier.

Facing Facts

Physical therapy may start very early in the life of a child diagnosed with cystic fibrosis, depending on their symptoms. Therapy may include clearing the airways to help loosen and remove mucus buildup and showing children how to maintain good posture to avoid back problems. If there are issues with the back and poor posture it can affect the lungs and their ability to work.

Physical therapists work with children to help them learn how to prevent problems with the way they stand and sit.

Understanding Cystic Fibrosis

Incontinence is when people accidentally leak some urine or release feces. This is embarrassing, but not unusual. It happens in around one in seven women in the United States. Urinary incontinence can be triggered by coughing or sneezing, which make abdominal muscles contract strongly and push on the bladder. If the pelvic floor muscles fail to keep the bladder closed, urine leaks out. Women with cystic fibrosis cough much more and much longer than usual, so they may have specialist physical therapy to learn "the knack." This is an exercise that involves tightening and lifting the pelvic floor muscles before coughing to protect against leaks.

Healthy Lifestyles

Medication and physical therapy are important ways to deal with the symptoms of cystic fibrosis. However, like all people, those with the disease can help their general health by being careful about what they eat and doing plenty of exercise.

Eating to Help Symptoms

Only about 10 percent of people with cystic fibrosis have a pancreas that can produce enough enzymes to digest their food properly. The rest cannot naturally get enough enzymes into their digestive system, so they take enzyme capsules with every meal and snack. People with cystic fibrosis often cannot digest and absorb fat and protein properly, so they have to eat a higher fat and protein diet than people without the disease.

A Different Diet

Healthcare professionals called dieticians also advise people with cystic fibrosis to eat twice as much food as people without the disease. This is because people with cystic fibrosis need to take in more energy to help them fight chest infections and build up their energy reserves to deal with weight loss during the frequent episodes of illness that they have. High-fiber diets, with plenty of vegetables and wholegrain bread or pasta, can also help reduce the symptoms of constipation and diarrhea. Eating calorie-rich foods such as nuts, seeds, avocados, and dairy products can help ensure people get the energy that they need, as well as the nutrients.

Swimming is a great exercise for people with cystic fibrosis.

Understanding Cystic Fibrosis

Exercise really helps people with cystic fibrosis. It helps keep the body fit and healthy so it can deal better with the condition. Exercises such as running, swimming, football, or tennis that make people feel out of breath are especially good. These help keep the lungs strong so they are better able to clear mucus. It's also important for people who have cystic fibrosis to keep their chests and shoulders flexible and relaxed, so they don't tighten up and make symptoms worse.

Physical therapists can show adults simple stretching exercises that can help keep their muscles flexible. Younger children can be encouraged to play games that involve lots of moving and stretching of the upper part of their body and arms.

Facing Facts

People with cystic fibrosis need regular monitoring by healthcare professionals to check their overall health.

Mental Health and Cystic Fibrosis

Managing a chronic illness is very difficult, and it is not surprising that people with cystic fibrosis find that the disease affects not only their physical health but their mental health too. The anxiety around risk of infection, fatigue, and a sense that life cannot be lived normally can lead to mental health issues.

LEADING TO ANXIETY

The worry of infection and the subsequent effect on a person's health can make people with cystic fibrosis extremely anxious for much of the time. The anxiety can lead to emotional exhaustion, which combined with the physical exhaustion people feel, can be extremely debilitating.

Worries about their health and the future can lead to issues with mental health for people with cystic fibrosis.

AN UNCERTAIN FUTURE

Cystic fibrosis can be an unpredictable disease. One of the few certainties about the condition is that it is progressive, which means it worsens with time. Dealing with the uncertainty of living with a chronic illness and facing future challenges, such as lung transplantation or worsening health, can lead to people becoming depressed about their current situation and what the future holds.

Physical Leads to Psychological

Managing cystic fibrosis can have a big impact on relationships with family, friends, and partners. The burden on people caring for loved ones with the disease is intense, as are concerns they may have about the future. The physical demands alone of caring for a person with cystic fibrosis are heavy. When added to the emotional stress that surrounds the disease, relationships between carers and the person they care for can become strained.

Dealing with cystic fibrosis is challenging both for the person with the disease and those that love and care for them.

Dealing with Mental Health

Although living with cystic fibrosis puts a huge strain on people with the disease and those who care for them, there are strategies that can improve mental wellbeing. Focusing on self-care can make a real difference to people's emotional health, and with the support of family, friends, and healthcare professionals, maintaining a positive frame of mind is possible.

MANAGING STRESS

Stress can feel overwhelming for people having to manage the unpredictable symptoms and uncertain future of cystic fibrosis. Strategies to manage stress have been shown to make dealing with a high-stress situation easier. They include relaxing exercises such as yoga, meditation, visualization, and deep-breathing exercises. Having nondraining, restorative hobbies such as listening to an audio book, music, podcasts, or watching a favorite television show are welcome distractions too when people are feeling low or anxious.

EATING FOR EMOTIONAL HEALTH

Focusing on a healthy lifestyle is key to helping manage both the physical and psychological effects of cystic fibrosis. Keeping up with a regular intake of food, supplements, and water, and exercising helps keep people as physically fit as possible, and also improves their mental wellbeing. Prioritizing self-care needs helps relieve some of the anxiety around achieving all of the many daily targets that surround nutrition and exercise for people with cystic fibrosis.

Taking time out to relax is an essential part of health and wellbeing.

PAYING ATTENTION

Healthcare professionals who work with people with cystic fibrosis recommend using mindfulness to help ease the anxiety that understandably often comes with the disease. Techniques that are helpful include:

Paying attention to sensation: noticing sensations in the body and if feeling discomfort, focusing on the sensation and noticing if it changes

Noticing emotions: focusing on what is felt at any one moment, and noting it

Music: picking a song and listening to the beat and the lyrics, or words of the song

Being able to relax when needed, without feeling under pressure to work or socialize, allows people with cystic fibrosis to give themselves the rest they need when their symptoms worsen.

Studies have shown that journaling is especially beneficial for young people with cystic fibrosis. It helps reduce anxiety, depression, and pain, and generally improves emotional resilience and wellbeing.

Some people find that talking with family and friends is not enough. A trained therapist can help people with the disease talk openly and honestly about their experiences, without fear of upsetting others.

CHAPTER 5

Living with Cystic Fibrosis

Everyone with cystic fibrosis is an individual with their own version of the disease and a unique range of symptoms. With advances in treatments, cystic fibrosis is no longer as limiting to people's lives as it was in the past. But for most people, it still affects their day-to-day lives in different ways. Cystic fibrosis is a life-changing disease, and life events experienced by people who do not have the disease are often not possible for people with the condition.

The Impact on Men

Almost all men who have cystic fibrosis are infertile. This means they cannot have their own children. Some men with cystic fibrosis may adopt children with their partners or they may have surgery or a special fertility treatment. This can sometimes help them have their own child.

Families may need therapy to help them learn to adapt to living with cystic fibrosis.

The Impact on Women

Most women who have cystic fibrosis can become pregnant without any problems. The difficulty for women is that being pregnant can make their symptoms worse. There is also the issue of passing on the gene for cystic fibrosis. If someone has cystic fibrosis, that means they have two defective copies of the CFTR gene and will pass one of those on to their child. The baby will either be a carrier or have the condition themselves, depending on the gene they get from the other parent. Some couples choose to have genetic testing to find out if the other partner is a carrier of the CFTR gene. This helps them make a decision about having children together.

Understanding Cystic Fibrosis

Unfortunately, cystic fibrosis tends to get worse over time. As people with the disease get older, their symptoms change and worsen. They may need to take more or different medications, and alter the physical therapy exercises they do or the other treatments they have. For example, people with cystic fibrosis are more likely to get a condition called osteoporosis, which is a thinning of the bones. When cystic fibrosis sufferers have osteoporosis, they may no longer be able to have percussion treatments because it might break their bones. As people get older, the effects of cystic fibrosis start to take their toll and people get weaker. Most people with cystic fibrosis do not live as long as those without the condition.

"It helps people to realize that some days will be worse than others, and vice versa. The disease brings many ups and downs, and sometimes people may feel more sick or tired than others. Simply accepting that can help people manage living with cystic fibrosis."

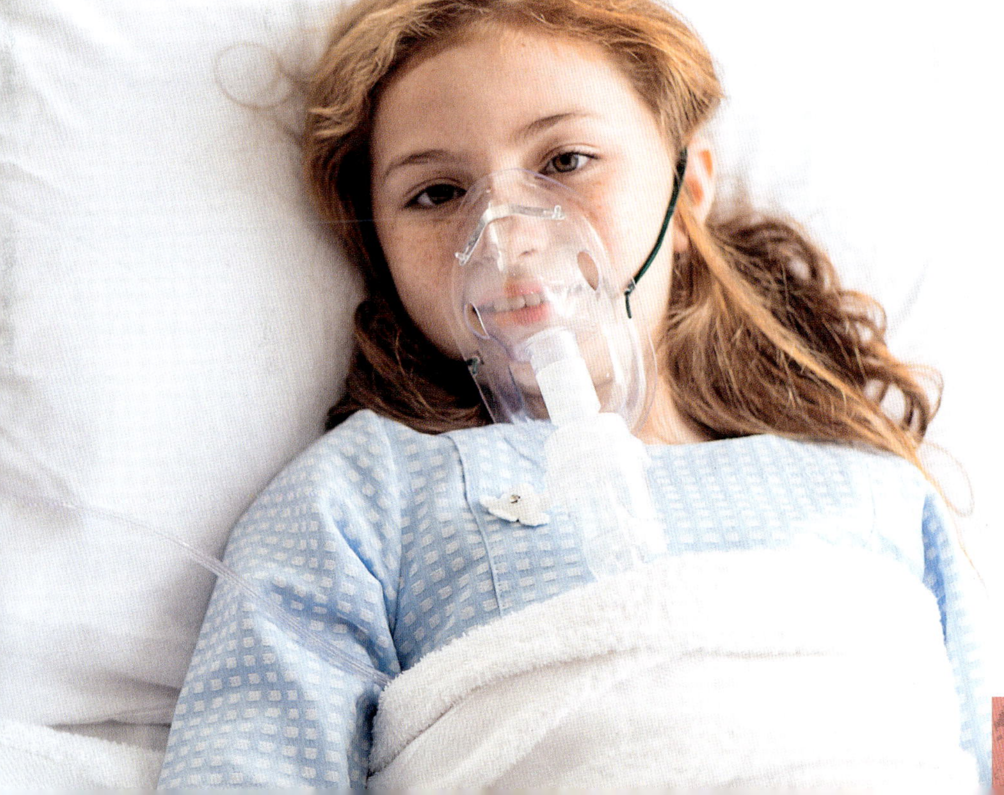

Pollen can be dangerous for people with cystic fibrosis and they must take care to avoid inhaling it.

A Plan for Dealing with Cystic Fibrosis

Today, there are better treatments for cystic fibrosis sufferers, so people with the condition are living longer than they did in the past. Longer lives, though, bring different challenges for people with the condition. As well as taking their medications, having physical therapy treatments, eating well, and exercising often, people with cystic fibrosis also have to care for themselves in other ways.

Strategies That Help

People with cystic fibrosis are at greater risk of getting lung infections than other people. When mucus builds up in their lungs, bacteria thrive and multiply. To protect themselves, people with the disease have to take precautions.

Avoiding germs: People with cystic fibrosis must be vigilant about avoiding germs, many of which are passed on by dirty hands. When people touch an object such as a doorknob that someone with an infection has touched, then put their hands in their mouth, bacteria get into their system. To prevent this, people with cystic fibrosis wash their hands carefully and often with warm soapy water or use a hand gel.

Reducing mucus buildup: Cystic fibrosis sufferers have to avoid anything that might cause them to make more mucus, because this will make their symptoms much worse. This has a surprising impact on their lives. For example, people with cystic fibrosis who have long hair never leave their hair wet, because the cold and damp would make their lungs produce more mucus.

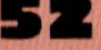

Avoiding irritants: All sufferers must avoid mold, smoke, and pollen because these substances are irritants and can lead to mucus buildup. This means that people with the disease have to be careful when they go outdoors, because mold is often found on plants, soil, or rotting vegetation. Pollen is a powder released by flowers and trees in summer, so extra care must be taken in the summer months.

Regular shots: As well as all the regular immunizations, people with cystic fibrosis must also get shots every year to stop them from getting the flu or pneumonia. They also try to avoid friends who have infectious illnesses until those friends have recovered.

Facing Facts

As children grow up, they must learn to take more responsibility for their own care and treatment. This helps them manage their condition if they go to college, get a job, and move away from home.

Young adulthood brings with it more responsibilities, including managing self-care and medical treatments.

Employment and Cystic Fibrosis

Working when you have cystic fibrosis is not easy. The daily medication, nutritional requirements, and rest required makes finding a suitable job difficult. Although the workplace is slowly becoming more accommodating of people with diseases and disorders, the challenges of finding and keeping a job for a person with cystic fibrosis are significant.

MANAGING THE CONDITION WHILE WORKING

The tiredness and reduced stamina that come with cystic fibrosis means that people have to manage their energy levels throughout the day. That often means that they need to pace themselves at work, take breaks as needed, and prioritize their eating plans to make sure they have enough energy and nutrients to function well. All of those requirements can limit the type of work available to people with the condition and exclude certain job roles in which taking regular breaks and rest would be impossible. A part-time role can be a good solution for people with cystic fibrosis. It means they can carry on working, while taking rest days to recover.

People with cystic fibrosis cannot do heavily physical jobs, such as those that require a lot of walking, standing, or lifting. Office-based jobs that are more sedentary are better options.

THE RISK OF WORKING

Going to a workplace where people mix with coworkers brings the risk of infection, which is always a concern for people with cystic fibrosis. Exposure to sick coworkers is not always avoidable, and if people with the condition become infected, it can be dangerous. If they become sick, their health can be greatly impacted and they will need time off work to recover. For those reasons, the threat of infection can make going out to work feel too risky for people with the condition.

Adding to the Stress

Finding it difficult to find a suitable job, being unable to work full-time, or not working due to fears about the health implications all have a financial impact on people with cystic fibrosis. They often cannot earn the same salary that a person without the disease might expect, and that puts financial strains on them and their family. The money worries that come as a result add to a person's already-high levels of anxiety.

Many service-based jobs, such as working in retail or in a café, are not suitable for people with cystic fibrosis because they are too tiring and pose too great a risk of infection.

Dealing with Employment

It is true that having cystic fibrosis makes it more difficult to find a suitable job, but it is also true that many people with the condition do find work that they enjoy and workplaces that they thrive in. Many people with cystic fibrosis want to work and are able to work. The key thing for them is finding a career that works around their health needs.

GETTING INTO WORK

Finding an employer willing to accommodate the health needs of a person with cystic fibrosis is often the key to getting work. Today, more employers than ever are open to making work more flexible for people. There are also support services that help link people with cystic fibrosis with suitable employers. The services screen employers to make sure they offer the following features at work:

- Remote working, or working from home
- Part-time and flexi-work
- Sitting down at work
- Health insurance plans
- Lifts in the workplace
- Supportive sick-leave policies
- Health and safety regulation around sanitation

Supportive and inclusive workplaces are better environments for people both with and without disabilities.

MAKING WORK WORKABLE

Putting in place smart strategies for maintaining a job helps people with cystic fibrosis keep healthy while working. That often includes making a schedule with time set aside for treatment, food, and exercise, all of which keep people fit for work. Being smart about making appointments also helps—scheduling hospital or doctor visits around lunch and other breaktimes reduces their impact on the working day.

Respect and Support

The benefits of working for people with cystic fibrosis are great. Work provides a sense of normality, a chance to socialize, a purpose, job satisfaction, improved self-esteem, and financial security. All of those positive benefits greatly improve mental health and quality of life. People with the condition have skills and contributions to bring to the workplace, so ensuring that they can do so is beneficial not only for those who deal with cystic fibrosis but also for their employers and coworkers.

Not overworking helps people stay at work. Working too hard for too long leads to exhaustion, sickness, and time off work, so is counterproductive.

Talking about the demands and difficulties of cystic fibrosis informs coworkers. They can then better support people with the disease.

Working from home when needed makes it easier for people to manage their health. Many people work from home during winter months when cold and flu infections are more common.

Cystic Fibrosis and the Future

Cystic fibrosis is a very serious disease that once was severely life limiting. In the past, people with cystic fibrosis would be lucky to live past five years old. Today, there are many more adults than children with cystic fibrosis. As a result of improved medical treatment, nutrition, physical therapy, and understanding of cystic fibrosis, many people with the condition live to be 50 or older, with a greater quality of life than ever before.

Improving on Gene Therapy

Scientists are getting closer to being able to offer safe, effective gene therapies to people with cystic fibrosis, often by building on established techniques. For example, some virus-based gene therapy effectively targets mutated genes, but the changes may not be permanent, so repeat therapy is needed. Additionally, gene editing can be very accurate in the laboratory, but the treatment is impractical for targeting cells hidden inside human bodies.

New Repair Therapy

The limitations of the two currently available approaches for gene therapy are being dealt with through second-generation gene repair. This therapy combines the gene delivery ability of viruses with the permanent gene-editing abilities of CRISPR/Cas9. The promise of second generation gene repair is that it can permanently correct the region of chromosome 7 containing the six most common CFTR mutations. These include Delta F508, and around 80 percent of the less-common mutations in people with cystic fibrosis.

Advances in supportive care, treatment, and research are helping people with cystic fibrosis lead fuller and longer lives.

"While challenges remain, the outlook for people with cystic fibrosis is far brighter today than it has ever been."

Understanding Cystic Fibrosis

In the near future, people with different cystic fibrosis variants will have access to different types of personalized healthcare. This will help them deal with their particular symptoms. Many therapies for cystic fibrosis treat general symptoms such as lung infection or lack of pancreatic enzymes. However, precision medicines directly target the causes of cystic fibrosis associated with particular variants. In these, chemicals interact with the faulty CFTR protein to make it work better. For example, ivacaftor helps open gates in cell membranes to let salt move more effectively. Gate mutations affect less than 10 percent of people with cystic fibrosis, so there is no point giving this medication to others who do not have such mutations. Another drug, lumacaftor, helps get more CFTR protein to the surface of cells, and is more suitable to people with other variants.

Glossary

accommodating willing to make adjustments in order to meet the needs of others

airborne transported through the air

amino acids important parts of protein

anxiety a state of fear or worry

bacteria tiny organisms that can cause infections or diseases

beneficial having a positive effect

chromosomal related to threadlike structures found in cells that carry genetic information

chronic diseases long-lasting or persistent diseases

conspicuous easily noticeable

contributions acts or things given that benefit others

counterproductive has the opposite effect to the one desired

depressed feeling sad and hopeless

descendants people who are related to people who lived before

detergent a cleaning solution

diagnosed identified the presence of a condition, illness, or disease

digestive system parts of the body that break down food, absorb nutrients, and remove waste

distract captures a person's attention so that they are no longer focused on a task

donated given

donor a person who gives part of their body to help others

embryo the early stage of development after fertilization of an egg cell by a sperm cell but before the organism becomes a fetus

enzymes proteins that help the body carry out chemical reactions, such as those needed to digest food

esophagus the tube that leads from the mouth to the stomach

ethical relating to values that are considered important, such as fairness and equality

excreted removed from the body

exhaled breathed out

extracurricular activities undertaken outside of regular academic or work responsibilities, such as sports, clubs, hobbies, and volunteer work

fetuses growing, unborn babies

fiber tough parts of foods such as vegetables needed for healthy digestion

financial security having enough money to live without concerns

fungi plantlike organisms, or living things

gallbladder a small organ in the body that stores bile, a liquid needed for digestion

immunizations injections given to protect the body against infections

impact having an influence or effect on something

inclusive encouraging the inclusion of diverse groups of people

inflates blows up with air

inhaling breathing in

intestines the long, tubelike organs of the digestive system

liver a large organ in the body that breaks down and removes waste

lung transplant the surgical removal of a healthy lung from one person and using it to replace an unhealthy lung in another person

membranes barriers between one thing and another

microscopic too small to be seen without the aid of a microscope

mobility the ability to move

nauseous feeling that one might vomit, or throw up

neurons nerve cells that pass messages around the body

nutrients substances needed for growth, development, and good health

organs body parts

overwhelmed feeling unable to cope

pancreas an organ in the body that makes pancreatic juice, a liquid needed for digestion

persistent continual and does not easily go away

pneumonia a dangerous infection of the lungs

pollen a fine powder produced by plants

radiation a fast-moving energy

regulation controls and rules

resilience the ability to adapt, recover, or bounce back from challenges or setbacks

sanitation related to cleanliness

sedentary mainly still and not moving often

self-esteem confidence in one's own worth or abilities

sequences regular arrangements that follow an order

sick-leave policies workplace rules related to pay and support given to a person when they are unable to work

simulate to show how something might work in practice

supplements dietary products containing vitamins, minerals, herbs, or other substances

symptoms the signs of illness or disease

umbilical cord the tube that connects an unborn baby to the placenta, an organ that provides the baby with all it needs to survive and grow

unpredictable difficult to estimate the likelihood of something

ventilated describes an area in which air moves freely

vigilant very careful

viral related to viruses, tiny infectious organisms that can replicate, or copy themselves, inside other organisms and cause disease

viruses tiny infectious organisms that can replicate, or copy themselves, inside other organisms and cause disease

Books

Finn, M. Dr Kelsey and Francesca Medenhall. *Having Cystic Fibrosis Is a Lot Like Being a Superhero.* Independently Published, 2020.

Hawkins, Carole. *Asthma, Cystic Fibrosis, and Other Respiratory Diseases* (Living with Diseases and Disorders). Mason Crest, 2017.

Mullan, Lisa. *My DNA Diary: Cystic Fibrosis* (Genetics for Kids). Dinky Press, 2018.

Websites

Find out more about cystic fibrosis at:
https://kidshealth.org/en/teens/cystic-fibrosis.html

Discover more about cystic fibrosis at:
www.cff.org/intro-cf/about-cystic-fibrosis

Learn all about cystic fibrosis at:
www.lung.org/lung-health-diseases/lung-disease-lookup/cystic-fibrosis/learn-about-cystic-fibrosis

Publisher's note to educators and parents:
All the websites featured above have been carefully reviewed to ensure that they are suitable for students. However, many websites change often, and we cannot guarantee that a site's future contents will continue to meet our high standards of educational value. Please be advised that students should be closely monitored whenever they access the Internet.

Index

About the Author

Sarah Eason has written many books for children and young adults. Researching and writing this book has highlighted the complex and demanding nature of cystic fibrosis, and the challenges that people with the condition face. She hopes this book is an informative, helpful, and compassionate resource for readers who are interested in the topic or affected by it.